PRAYERS

of a

Dedicated TEACHER

PRAYERS

of a

Dedicated **TEACHER**

THIRD EDITION

The quoted ideas expressed in this book (but not Scripture verses) are not, in all cases, exact quotations, as some have been edited for clarity and brevity. In all cases, the author has attempted to maintain the speaker's original intent. In some cases, quoted material for this book was obtained from secondary sources, primarily print media. While every effort was made to ensure the accuracy of these sources, the accuracy cannot be guaranteed. For additions, deletions, corrections, or clarifications in future editions of this text, please write Brighton Books.

The Holy Bible, New International Version (NIV) Copyright © 1973, 1978, 1984, by International Bible Society. Used by permission of Zondervan Publishing House. All rights reserved.

The Holy Bible, New King James Version (NKJV) Copyright © 1982 by Thomas Nelson, Inc. Used by permission.

The Holy Bible, New Living Translation (NLT) Copyright © 1996. Used by permission of Tyndale House Publishers, Incorporated, Wheaton, Illinois 60189. All rights reserved.

The New American Standard Bible®, (NASB) Copyright © 1960, 1962, 1963, 1968, 1971, 1972, 1973, 1975, 1977, 1995 by The Lockman Foundation. Used by permission.

The Holman Christian Standard Bible™ (HCSB) Copyright © 1999, 2000, 2001 by Holman Bible Publishers. Used by permission.

Cover design & page layout by: Bart Dawson
Copy written and compiled by: Criswell Freeman

ISBN 1-58334-209-5
        1 2 3 4 5 6 7 8 9 10 • 03 04 05 06 07 08 09 10

Printed in the United States of America

Contents

Introduction   10

A Prayer for . . .

  1. Those Who Teach   13

  2. God's Grace   17

  3. God's Wisdom   21

  4. Patience   25

  5. Hope for the Future   29

  6. Strength   33

  7. An Encouraging Heart   37

My Hopes & Prayers for Next Week   41

  8. Perseverance   43

  9. Understanding   47

  10. A Righteous Heart   51

  11. Courage   55

  12. A Compassionate Heart   59

  13. The Wisdom to Lead   63

  14. A Disciplined Heart   67

My Hopes & Prayers for Next Week   71

  15. A Godly Attitude   73

A Prayer for . . .

16. Strength in Adversity 77

17. Spiritual Abundance 81

18. A Joyful Heart 85

19. Confidence 89

20. The Courage to Discipline 93

21. A Generous Spirit 97

My Hopes & Prayers for Next Week 101

22. The Wisdom to Laugh 103

23. Words That Are Pleasing to God 107

24. Optimism and Faith 111

25. A Thankful Heart 115

26. A Forgiving Heart 119

27. A Trusting Heart 123

28. Renewal 127

My Hopes & Prayers for Next Week 131

29. Today 133

30. Our Children 137

31. God's Love 141

My Hopes & Prayers for Next Month 145

Selected Scripture 149

Introduction

Henry Adams correctly observed, "A teacher affects eternity; he can never tell where his influence stops." And, those words have never been more true than they are today. We live in a difficult, fast-paced, temptation-filled world; more than ever, our young people need the direction and the leadership provided by teachers who know and love God.

This book contains devotional reading for Christians who teach. The text is divided into 31 chapters, one for each day of the month. During the next 31 days, please try this experiment: read a chapter each day. If you're already committed to a daily worship time, this book will enrich that experience. If you are not, the simple act of giving God a few minutes each morning will change the direction and the quality of your life.

Whether you teach graduate school or Sunday School, whether you lecture at seminary or at Vacation Bible School, you need and deserve a regularly scheduled conference with the ultimate Teacher. After all, you are God's emissary, a person charged with molding lives.

God takes your teaching duties very seriously, and so should you.

So, if you are fortunate enough to find yourself in the role of teacher, accept a hearty congratulations and a profound word of thanks. And then, take a few moments to consider the promises and prayers on these pages. Remember that God honors your profession just as surely as He offers His loving abundance to you and your students. With God's help, you are destined to reshape eternity. It's a big job, but don't worry: You and God, working together, can handle it.

Day 1
A Prayer for . . .

Those Who Teach

Fix these words of mine in your hearts and minds.
Teach them to your children, talking about them
when you sit at home and when you walk along
the road, when you lie down and when you get up.

Deuteronomy 11:18-19 NIV

As a teacher, your profession places you in a position of profound responsibility: you help mold the minds and lives of your students. Daniel Webster wrote, "If we work in marble, it will perish; if we work upon brass, time will efface it; if we rear temples, they will crumble into dust; but if we work upon immortal minds and instill in them just principles, we are then engraving upon tablets which no time will efface, but which will brighten and brighten to all eternity." These words remind us of the glorious opportunities that are available to those of us who teach.

Being a godly teacher in today's difficult world requires insight, discipline, patience, and prayer. May you, with God's help, touch the hearts and minds of your students and, in doing so, refashion this wonderful world . . . and the next.

It is desirable that children be kind,
appreciative and pleasant.
Those qualities should be taught
and not hoped for.

James Dobson

If you want to be a teacher, remember that
you're just as likely to teach who you are
as you are to teach what you know.

Marie T. Freeman

Let us look upon our children; let us love them
and train them as children of the covenant
and children of the promise.
These are the children of God.

Andrew Murray

Be gentle to all, able to teach, patient.

2 Timothy 2:24 NKJV

Dear Lord, there is so much to teach and
so little time. Let me share Your wisdom
with my students, with my family,
and with the world. And, let my love for
You be evident in the lessons that I teach
and the life that I live.

—Amen—

My Prayer for Today

A Prayer for . . .

God's Grace

For by grace you have been saved through faith,
and that not of yourselves; it is the gift of God.

Ephesians 2:8 NKJV

Christ sacrificed His life on the cross so that we might have life eternal. This gift, freely given from God's only begotten Son, is the priceless possession of everyone who accepts Him as Lord and Savior. Thankfully, grace is not an earthly reward for righteous behavior; it is, instead, a blessed spiritual gift. When we accept Christ into our hearts, we are saved by His grace.

The familiar words from the Book of Ephesians make God's promise perfectly clear: "It is by grace you have been saved . . . not by works, so that no one can boast" (2:8-9 NIV). God's grace is the ultimate gift, and we owe Him the ultimate in thanksgiving. Let us praise the Creator for His priceless gift, and let us share the Good News with friends, family members, students, and the world.

We return our Father's love by accepting His grace and by sharing His message and His love. When we do, we are eternally blessed. God is waiting patiently for each of us to accept the gift of eternal life. Let us claim His gift today.

We are here to be living monuments
to God's grace.

Oswald Chambers

Let us then approach the throne of grace
with confidence, so that we may receive mercy
and find grace to help us in our time of need.

Hebrews 4:16 NIV

The will of God will never lead you where
the grace of God cannot keep you.

Warren Wiersbe

God does amazing works through prayers
that seek to extend His grace to others.

Shirley Dobson

Lord, You have saved me by Your grace.
Keep me mindful that Your grace is a gift that
I can accept but cannot earn. I praise You for
that priceless gift, today and forever.
Let me share the Good News of Your grace
with a world that desperately needs
Your healing touch.
—Amen—

My Prayer for Today

Day 3

A Prayer for . . .

God's Wisdom

Know that wisdom is sweet to your soul;
if you find it, there is a future hope for you,
and your hope will not be cut off.

Proverbs 24:14 NIV

As a thoughtful teacher, you certainly understand the value of education. And, as a prayerful Christian, you know the value of God's wisdom. Knowledge can be found in textbooks. Wisdom, on the other hand, is found in God's Holy Word and in the carefully chosen words of loving parents and dedicated teachers.

When you share the gift of knowledge with your students, you have done them a wonderful service. But, when you share the gift of wisdom—by your words and by your example—you have offered a timeless treasure that has the power to reshape the lives of your students.

Today, as you go about the business of molding the hearts and minds of your students, remember that your task, as a dedicated teacher, is to share both knowledge and wisdom. But not necessarily in that order.

He who walks with the wise grows wise . . . .

Proverbs 13:20 NIV

If you lack knowledge, go to school.
If you lack wisdom, get on your knees.

Vance Havner

Don't expect wisdom to come into your
life like great chunks of rock on a conveyor
belt. Wisdom comes privately from God as a
byproduct of right decisions, godly reactions,
and the application of spiritual principles
to daily circumstances.

Charles Swindoll

The man who prays ceases to be a fool.

Oswald Chambers

Dear Lord, make me a teacher of wisdom
and discernment. Lead me in Your ways
and teach me from Your Word so that,
in time, my wisdom might glorify
Your kingdom and Your Son.
—Amen—

My Prayer for Today

A Prayer for . . .

Patience

Be gentle to all, able to teach, patient.
2 Timothy 2:24 KJV

The teaching profession requires heaping helpings of patience, understanding, forgiveness, and poise. Sometimes, students are impulsive; sometimes, they misbehave; oftentimes, students under-perform; sometimes, they simply don't show up at all.

Despite the inevitable shortcomings of their students, savvy teachers maintain their composure—even when students or parents don't.

Our world is filled with imperfect people; so are our classrooms. All of us, students and faculty members alike, make our share of mistakes. God commands us to respond to the shortcomings of others with patience, understanding, forgiveness, and love—which, by the way, is exactly how God has already responded to us.

Grass that is here today and gone tomorrow
does not require much time to mature.
A big oak tree that lasts for generations requires
much more time to grow and mature.
God is concerned about your life through
eternity. Allow Him to take all the time
He needs to shape you for His purposes.
Larger assignments will require
longer periods of preparation.

Henry Blackaby

If you want to hear God's voice clearly and
you are uncertain, then remain in His presence
until He changes that uncertainty. Often much
can happen during this waiting for the Lord.
Sometimes he changes pride into humility;
doubt into faith and peace.

Corrie ten Boom

Rest in the LORD, and wait patiently for Him.

Psalm 37:7 NKJV

Dear Lord, help me to understand the wisdom
of patience. When I am hurried, slow me down.
When I become impatient with others,
give me empathy. Today, let me be a patient
servant and a patient teacher, as I serve You
and bring glory to Your Son.
—Amen—

My Prayer for Today

Day 5
A Prayer for . . .

Hope
for the
Future

Let us hold fast the confession of
our hope without wavering,
for He who promised is faithful.
Hebrews 10:23 NASB

In these uncertain times, it's easy to lose hope for the future . . . but it's wrong. God instructs us to trust His wisdom, His plan, and His love. When we do so, the future becomes a glorious opportunity to help others, to praise our Creator, and to share God's Good News.

Do you have faith in the ultimate goodness of God's plan? You should. And, do you have faith in the abundant opportunities that await your students? Hopefully, you do. After all, the confidence that you display in your students can be contagious: Your belief in them can have a profound impact on the way they view themselves and their world.

Today, as you stand before your classroom, help your students face the future with optimism, hope, and self-confidence. After all, even in these uncertain times, God still has the last word. And His love endures to all generations, including this one.

Teach us to set our hopes on heaven,
to hold firmly to the promise of eternal life,
so that we can withstand the struggles
and storms of this world.

Max Lucado

Never be afraid to trust an unknown future
to an all-knowing God.

Corrie ten Boom

For I know the thoughts that I think toward
you, says the LORD, thoughts of peace
and not of evil, to give you a future and a hope.
Then you will call upon Me and go
and pray to Me, and I will listen to you.

Jeremiah 29:11-12 NKJV

The essence of optimism is that it takes no
account of the present, but it is a source of
inspiration, of vitality, and of hope. Where
others have resigned, it enables a man to hold
his head high, to claim the future for himself,
and not abandon it to his enemy.

Dietrich Bonhoeffer

Dear Lord, as I look to the future, I will place
my trust in You. If I become discouraged,
I will turn to You. If I am afraid, I will seek
strength in You. You are my Father,
and I will place my hope, my trust,
and my faith in You.
—Amen—

My Prayer for Today

Day 6

A Prayer for . . .

Strength

I am able to do all things through
Him who strengthens me.
Philippians 4:13 HCSB

If you're a teacher with too many obligations and too few hours in which to meet them, you are not alone: yours is a demanding profession. As a dedicated teacher, you may experience moments when you feel overworked, overstressed, and under-appreciated. Thankfully, God stands ready to renew your optimism and your strength if you turn to Him.

When you feel worried or weary, focus your thoughts upon God and upon His love for you. Then, ask Him for the wisdom to prioritize your life and the strength to fulfill your responsibilities. God will give you the energy to do the most important things on today's to-do list . . . if you ask Him. So ask Him.

One with God is a majority.

Billy Graham

The LORD is my strength and my song . . . .

Exodus 15:2 NIV

We are never stronger than
the moment we admit we are weak.

Beth Moore

God is the One who provides our strength,
not only to cope with the demands of the day,
but also to rise above them. May we look to
Him for the strength to soar.

Jim Gallery

Dear Lord, let me turn to You for strength.
When I am weak, You lift me up. When
I am worried, You comfort me. When I am
victorious, Your Word reminds me to be
humble. Today and every day, I will turn
to You, Father, for strength, for hope,
for wisdom, and for salvation.

—Amen—

My Prayer for Today

A Prayer for . . .

An Encouraging Heart

Let us consider how to stimulate one another
to love and good deeds.

Hebrews 10:24 NASB

In the classroom, we encounter a specific category of people who desperately need our encouraging words: those people are called students—all students. And, as dedicated teachers, we must find creative ways to encourage them.

Today's world can be a difficult and uncertain place, especially for young people. Many of our students are in desperate need of a smile or an encouraging word, and since we don't always know who needs our help, the best strategy is to encourage all those who cross our paths. So today, as you address a classroom, be an enthusiastic booster and a proponent of possibilities. Who knows? Your encouraging words might just change someone's day . . . or someone's life.

A lot of people have gone further than they thought they could because someone else thought they could.

Zig Ziglar

Encouragement is the oxygen of the soul.

John Maxwell

It is helpful to remember the distinction between appreciation and affirmation. We appreciate what a person does, but we affirm who a person is.

Charles Swindoll

God has given each of us the ability to do certain things well. So if God has given you the ability to prophesy, speak out when you have faith that God is speaking through you. If your gift is that of serving others, serve them well. If you are a teacher, do a good job of teaching. If your gift is to encourage others, do it! If you have money, share it generously. If God has given you leadership ability, take the responsibility seriously. And if you have a gift for showing kindness to others, do it gladly.

Romans 12:6-8 NLT

A Prayer for Today

Dear Father, make me an encouraging teacher.
Just as You have lifted me up, let me also lift
up my students in the spirit of encouragement
and hope. Today, let me help my students find
the strength and the courage to use their gifts
according to Your master plan.

—Amen—

My Prayer for Today

My Hopes & Prayers for Next Week

My Hopes & Prayers for Next Week

A Prayer for . . .

Perseverance

For you need endurance, so that after
you have done God's will,
you may receive what was promised.

Hebrews 10:36 HCSB

The teaching profession is a marathon not a sprint. Sometimes, our students are attentive and responsive; at other times, our students are rebellious or apathetic. Some days, we teachers feel invigorated, enthusiastic, and authoritative; on other days, we may feel ill-equipped for the task at hand. But, on good days and bad ones, our students inevitably file into the classroom, and for better or worse we must teach.

Teaching requires perseverance, especially on those difficult days when the students are in an uproar and the lesson plan is in disarray. But, our Savior, Christ Jesus, finished what He began, and so must we. Sometimes, God answers our prayers with silence, and when He does, we must patiently persevere. In times of trouble, we must seek God through prayer and lean upon His strength. Whatever our problems, He can handle them. Our job is to keep persevering until He does.

Stand still and refuse to retreat.
Look at it as God looks at it and draw upon
His power to hold up under the blast.

Charles Swindoll

All rising to a great place is by a winding stair.

Francis Bacon

I do not consider myself yet to have taken hold
of it. But one thing I do: Forgetting what is
behind and straining toward what is ahead,
I press on toward the goal to win the prize
for which God has called me heavenward
in Christ Jesus.

Philippians 3:13-14 NIV

Jesus taught that perseverance is
the essential element in prayer.

E. M. Bounds

Lord, when life is difficult, I am tempted to abandon hope in the future. But You are my God, and I can draw strength from You. Let me trust You, Father, in good times and in bad times. Let me persevere—even if my soul is troubled—and let me follow Your Son Jesus Christ this day and forever.

—Amen—

My Prayer for Today

Day 9
A Prayer for . . .
Understanding

The wisdom that is from above is first pure,
then peaceable, gentle, and easy to be entreated,
full of mercy and good fruits, without partiality,
and without hypocrisy.

James 3:17 KJV

Because we are teachers, we must grade our students based upon their performance and their conduct. But as Christians, we must be careful that we not judge our students, or, for that matter, condemn them when they fall short. The distinction between grading and judging is subtle, but, for Christians, important. Grading students is our job; judging them is God's job.

All of us have fallen short of God's commandments, and He has forgiven us. We, too, must forgive others when they fall short. And, we must refrain from judging them.

As Christian believers, we are warned that to judge others is to invite fearful consequences: to the extent we judge others, so, too, will we be judged by God. Let us refrain, then, from judging our students, our neighbors, our family members, or our friends. Instead, let us love them and leave the judging to a far higher and far more capable authority.

The last and greatest lesson that the soul has
to learn is the fact that God, and God alone,
is enough for all its needs. This is the lesson
that all His dealings with us are meant to teach;
and this is the crowning discovery of our whole
Christian life. God is enough!

Hannah Whitall Smith

———

Trust in the LORD with all your heart;
do not depend on your own understanding.

Proverbs 3:5 NLT

———

The only Being who understands me
is the Being who made me.

Oswald Chambers

———

I pray that your love for each other
will overflow more and more, and that you
will keep on growing in your knowledge
and understanding.

Philippians 1:9 NLT

A Prayer for Today

Dear Lord, make me a compassionate Christian.
Fill me with wisdom, discernment,
and understanding. When I am tempted
to judge others harshly, give me a spirit of
forgiveness, knowing that ultimately
judgment is Yours and Yours alone.
—Amen—

My Prayer for Today

A Prayer for . . .

A Righteous Heart

Walk in a manner worthy of the God
who calls you into His own kingdom and glory.

1 Thessalonians 2:12 NASB

Like it or not, we teachers are role models, and we should conduct ourselves accordingly. We teach our students not only by the words we speak but also by the lives we live. That's why, as teachers, we must make certain that the lives we lead are in harmony with the lessons we teach.

Are you the kind of teacher whose life serves as a powerful example of righteousness and godliness? If so, you are also an enduring force for good in your classroom and in your world.

D. L. Moody advised, "More depends upon my walk than upon my talk." And that's sound advice because our students are watching . . . and so, for that matter, is God.

In our faith we leave footprints to guide others.
A child, a friend, a recent convert.
None should be left to walk the trail alone.

Max Lucado

Have your heart right with Christ, and he will
visit you often, and so turn weekdays
into Sundays, meals into sacraments,
homes into temples, and earth into heaven.

C. H. Spurgeon

If we have the true love of God in our hearts,
we will show it in our lives. We will not have to
go up and down the earth proclaiming it.
We will show it in everything we say or do.

D. L. Moody

He who pursues righteousness and love
finds life, prosperity and honor.

Proverbs 21:21 NIV

Dear Lord, let me be a righteous example to
my students. Let me be honest and good,
patient and kind, faithful to You and
loving to others . . . now and forever.
—Amen—

My Prayer for Today

A Prayer for . . .

Courage

But He said to them, "Why are you fearful,
you of little faith?" Then He got up
and rebuked the winds and the sea.
And there was a great calm.

Matthew 8:26 HCSB

Teaching is not for sissies! Standing before a classroom of inquisitive students can be a daunting task, especially for beginning instructors. Thankfully, when we are fearful, whether inside the classroom or out, there is a source from which we can gather courage and strength. That source is God.

Believing Christians have every reason to be courageous. After all, the ultimate battle has already been fought and won on the cross at Calvary. So the next time you find your courage tested to the limit, remember that God is as near as your next breath, and remember that He offers salvation to His children. He is your shield and your strength; He is your protector and your deliverer. Call upon Him in your hour of need and then be comforted. Whatever your challenge, whatever your trouble, God can handle it. And will.

Be strong and courageous, and do the work.
Don't be afraid or discouraged by the size of
the task, for the LORD God, my God,
is with you. He will not fail you or forsake you.

1 Chronicles 28:20 NLT

What is courage? It is the ability to be strong
in trust, in conviction, in obedience.
To be courageous is to step out in faith—
to trust and obey, no matter what.

Kay Arthur

When once we are assured that God is good,
then there can be nothing left to fear.

Hannah Whitall Smith

Seeing that a Pilot steers the ship in which we
sail, who will never allow us to perish even in
the midst of shipwrecks, there is no reason why
our minds should be overwhelmed with fear
and overcome with weariness.

John Calvin

Dear Lord, sometimes I face challenges that leave me worried and afraid. When I am fearful, let me seek Your strength. When I am anxious, give me faith. Keep me mindful, Lord, that You are my God. With You by my side, Lord, I have nothing to fear today, tomorrow, or forever.

—Amen—

My Prayer for Today

A Prayer for . . .

A Compassionate Heart

So, as those who have been chosen of God,
holy and beloved, put on a heart of compassion,
kindness, humility, gentleness and patience.

Colossians 3:12 NASB

Amid the countless demands of a teacher's busy day, it is easy to become frustrated. We are imperfect human beings struggling to manage our lives as best we can, but sometimes we fall short. When we are distracted or disappointed, we may neglect to share a kind word or a kind deed. This oversight hurts others, and it hurts us as well.

The words of Ephesians 4:32 remind us to "be kind to one another, tenderhearted, forgiving one another, just as God in Christ forgave you" (NKJV). When we share a word of encouragement with a student or extend the hand of friendship to a peer, God promises His blessings. But when we ignore the needs of others—or mistreat them—we risk God's retribution.

Today, be alert for those who need your smile, your kind words, or your helping hand. Make kindness a centerpiece of your dealings with others. They will be blessed, and so, too, will you.

Our Lord worked with people as they were,
and He was patient—not tolerant of sin,
but compassionate.

Vance Havner

We must learn to regard people less in
the light of what they do or do not do,
and more in the light of what they suffer.

Dietrich Bonhoeffer

Finally, all of you be of one mind, having
compassion for one another; love as brothers,
be tenderhearted, be courteous.

1 Peter 3:8 NKJV

It is when we come to the Lord in
our nothingness, our powerlessness and
our helplessness that He then enables us
to love in a way which, without Him,
would be absolutely impossible.

Elisabeth Elliot

Lord, make me a loving, encouraging,
compassionate Christian. And, let my love
for Christ be reflected through the kindness
that I show to my students, to my family,
to my friends, and to all who need
the healing touch of the Master's hand.
—Amen—

My Prayer for Today

A Prayer for . . .

The Wisdom to Lead

We have different gifts, according to the grace given us. If a man's gift is prophesying, let him use it in proportion to his faith. If it is serving, let him serve; if it is teaching, let him teach; if it is encouraging, let him encourage; if it is contributing to the needs of others, let him give generously; if it is leadership, let him govern diligently; if it is showing mercy, let him do it cheerfully.

Romans 12:6-8 NIV

As a teacher, you are automatically placed in a position of leadership. Unless you assume firm control over your students, effective learning will not take place in your classroom.

John Maxwell writes, "Great leaders understand that the right attitude will set the right atmosphere, which enables the right response from others." As the leader of your class, it's up to you to set the proper balance between discipline and amusement, between entertainment and scholarship.

Savvy teachers learn to strike an appropriate balance between discipline (which is necessary for maintaining order) and fun (which is necessary for maintaining interest). The rest, of course, is up to the students.

Those who are wise will shine like
the brightness of the heavens, and those
who lead many to righteousness,
like the stars for ever and ever.

Daniel 12:3 NIV

Wise people listen to wise instruction,
especially instruction from the Word of God.

Warren Wiersbe

It is amazing what will happen in
your leadership when you do not gauge
the happiness of your life or the greatness
of your day by how easy it was.

John Maxwell

But the wisdom that is from above is first pure,
then peaceable, gentle, willing to yield,
full of mercy and good fruits,
without partiality and without hypocrisy.

James 3:17 NKJV

A Prayer for Today

Dear Lord, let me be a leader in my classroom
and a worthy example to my students.
Give me wisdom, courage, compassion,
and faith. Let me turn to You, Father,
for guidance and for strength in all
that I say and do.
—Amen—

My Prayer for Today

Day 14

A Prayer for . . .

A
Disciplined
Heart

Discipline yourself for the purpose of godliness.

1 Timothy 4:7 NASB

As teachers, we demand discipline from our students. We must demand the same from ourselves.

When we study God's Holy Word, we are confronted again and again with God's intention that His children lead disciplined lives. God doesn't reward laziness. To the contrary, He expects believers to be diligent, energetic, and disciplined. God's message is clear: we must do our work first, and then we can expect a bountiful harvest. But we should never expect the harvest to precede the labor.

If you seek to be a force for good in the classroom, carry out your teaching duties in an organized, disciplined fashion: be prompt, be prepared, and be professional. Your example will demonstrate that discipline works . . . and then, hopefully, your students will, too.

The alternative to discipline is disaster.

Vance Havner

For God did not give us a spirit of timidity,
but a spirit of power, of love
and of self-discipline.

2 Timothy 1:7 NIV

True willpower and courage are not on
the battlefield, but in everyday conquests over
our inertia, laziness, and boredom.

D. L. Moody

If one examines the secret behind
a championship football team, a magnificent
orchestra, or a successful business,
the principal ingredient is invariably discipline.

James Dobson

A Prayer for Today

Heavenly Father, make me a diligent teacher
in the service of Your Son, Christ Jesus.
Let me teach others by the faithfulness of
my conduct, and let me follow Your will
and Your Word, today and every day.
—Amen—

My Prayer for Today

My Hopes & Prayers for Next Week

My Hopes & Prayers for Next Week

A Prayer for . . .

A Godly Attitude

Finally brothers, whatever is true, whatever is
honorable, whatever is just, whatever is pure,
whatever is lovely, whatever is commendable—
if there is any moral excellence and if there is
any praise—dwell on these things.

Philippians 4:8 HCSB

As the leader of your classroom, you must beware: your attitudes are contagious. If you're upbeat and optimistic, your students will tend to emulate you. But, if you fall prey to cynicism or pessimism, many of your students will, too.

How will you direct your thoughts today? Will you obey the words of Philippians 4:8 by dwelling upon those things that are honorable, true, and worthy of praise? Or will you allow your thoughts to be hijacked by the negativity that seems to dominate our troubled world? Are you fearful, angry, bored, or worried? Are you so preoccupied with the concerns of this day that you fail to thank God for the promise of eternity? Are you confused, bitter, or pessimistic? If so, God wants to have a little talk with you.

God intends that you experience joy and abundance, but He will not force His joy upon you; you must claim it for yourself. So, today and every day hereafter, focus your thoughts and your energies upon "whatever is commendable." Celebrate life, and before you know it, you'll find many of your students are joining in the celebration.

Attitude is all-important. Let the soul take
a quiet attitude of faith and love toward God,
and from there on, the responsibility is God's.
He will make good on His commitments.

A. W. Tozer

The things we think are the things that feed
our souls. If we think on pure and lovely things,
we shall grow pure and lovely like them;
and the converse is equally true.

Hannah Whitall Smith

For the word of God is living and active.
Sharper than any double-edged sword,
it penetrates even to dividing soul and spirit,
joints and marrow; it judges the thoughts
and attitudes of the heart.

Hebrews 4:12 NIV

The way you see life will largely determine
what you get out of it.

Zig Ziglar

Dear Lord, let me live my life and love my family with a spirit of hope and thanksgiving. And, let me teach my students—by my words and my deeds—that the Christian life is a life of optimism and trust. Whatever circumstances I face, whether good or bad, triumphal or tragic, let my response reflect a God-honoring, Christlike attitude of faith and love for You.
—Amen—

My Prayer for Today

Day 16

A Prayer for . . .

Strength in Adversity

God is our refuge and strength, always ready
to help in times of trouble. So we will
not fear, even if earthquakes come
and mountains crumble to the sea.

Psalm 46:1-2 NLT

From time to time, all of us face adversity, discouragement, or disappointment. And throughout our lives, we all must endure earthshaking personal losses that leave us breathless and feeling alone; turning to God is the only answer. When we do, He stands ready to protect us. Psalm 147 assures us that "He heals the brokenhearted, and binds their wounds" (v. 3 NIV).

Are you anxious? Take those anxieties to God. Are you troubled? Take your troubles to Him. Does the world seem to be trembling beneath your feet? Seek protection from the One who cannot be moved.

The same God who created the universe stands ready and willing to comfort you and to restore your strength. During life's most difficult days, your Heavenly Father remains steadfast. And, in His own time and according to His master plan, He will heal you if you invite Him into your heart.

But I will sing of your strength, in the morning
I will sing of your love; for you are my fortress,
my refuge in times of trouble.

Psalm 59:16 NIV

Measure the size of the obstacles
against the size of God.

Beth Moore

Weave the unveiling fabric of God's Word
through your heart and mind. It will hold
strong, even if the rest of life unravels.

Gigi Graham Tchividjian

The closer we are to God, the more confidence
we place in him when we are under fire.

C. H. Spurgeon

A Prayer for Today

Heavenly Father, You are my strength and
my refuge. As I journey through this day,
I know that I may encounter disappointments
and losses. When I am troubled, let me turn to
You. Keep me steady, Lord, and renew a right
spirit inside of me this day and forever.

—Amen—

My Prayer for Today

Day 17

A Prayer for . . .

Spiritual Abundance

I am come that they might have life,
and that they might have it more abundantly.

John 10:10 KJV

When Jesus describes the abundant life (John 10:10), is He talking about material riches or earthly fame? Hardly. The Son of God came to this world not to give it prosperity but to give it salvation. Thankfully, for Christians, our Savior's abundance is both spiritual and eternal; it never falters—even if we do—and it never dies. We need only to open our hearts to Him, and His grace becomes ours.

God's gifts are available to all, but those gifts are not guaranteed; God's gifts must be claimed by those who choose to follow Christ. As we go about our daily lives, inside the classroom and out, may we accept God's promise of spiritual abundance, and may we share it with a world in desperate need of the Master's healing touch.

We honor God by asking for great things when they are a part of His promise. We dishonor Him and cheat ourselves when we ask for molehills where He has promised mountains.

Vance Havner

Ask and it will be given to you; seek and you will find; knock and the door will be opened to you. For everyone who asks receives; he who seeks finds; and to him who knocks, the door will be opened.

Matthew 7:7-8 NIV

If we were given all we wanted here, our hearts would settle for this world rather than the next.

Elisabeth Elliot

People, places, and things were never meant to give us life. God alone is the author of a fulfilling life.

Gary Smalley & John Trent

Thank You, Father, for the abundant life that is
mine through Christ Jesus. Guide me according
to Your will, and help me to be a worthy servant
through all that I say and do. Give me courage,
Lord, to claim the rewards You have promised,
and when I do, let all the glory be Yours.

—Amen—

My Prayer for Today

Day 18
A Prayer for . . .

A Joyful Heart

This is the day the LORD has made;
let us rejoice and be glad in it.

Psalm 118:24 NIV

Teaching can and should be a joyful experience. Of course, as every veteran teacher knows, some days are more challenging than others. But even on the most difficult days, we can find pockets of satisfaction, islands of peace, and moments of joy.

Psalm 100 reminds us that, as believers, we have every reason to celebrate: "Shout for joy to the LORD, all the earth. Worship the LORD with gladness" (v. 1-2 NIV). Yet sometimes, amid the inevitable hustle and bustle of life here on earth, we can forfeit—albeit temporarily—the joy that God intends for our lives. C. H. Spurgeon, the renowned nineteenth-century English clergymen, advised, "Rejoicing is clearly a spiritual command. To ignore it, I need to remind you, is disobedience." As Christians, we are called by our Creator to live abundantly, prayerfully, and joyfully. To do otherwise is to squander His spiritual gifts.

If, today, your heart is heavy, open the door of your soul to the Father and to His Son. Christ offers you His peace and His joy. Accept it and share it freely, just as Christ has freely shared His joy with you.

God knows everything. He can manage
everything, and He loves us.
Surely this is enough for a fullness
of joy that is beyond words.

Hannah Whitall Smith

I choose joy. I will refuse the temptation to be
cynical; cynicism is the tool of a lazy thinker.
I will refuse to see people as anything less than
human beings, created by God. I will refuse
to see any problem as anything less
than an opportunity to see God.

Max Lucado

Joy is the serious business of heaven.

C. S. Lewis

I will thank you, LORD, with all my heart;
I will tell of all the marvelous things you have
done. I will be filled with joy because of you.
I will sing praises to your name, O Most High.

Psalm 9:1-2 NLT

Dear Lord, You have given me so many
blessings; let me celebrate Your gifts.
Make me thankful, loving, responsible,
and wise. I praise you, Father, for the gift of
Your Son and for the priceless gift of salvation.
Make me a joyful Christian, a worthy example
to others, and a dutiful servant
to You this day and forever.
—Amen—

My Prayer for Today

Day 19

A Prayer for . . .

Confidence

Therefore I tell you, do not worry about
your life, what you will eat or drink; or about
your body, what you will wear. Is not life more
important than food, and the body more
important than clothes? Look at the birds of
the air; they do not sow or reap or store away in
barns, and yet your heavenly Father feeds them.
Are you not much more valuable than they?

Matthew 6:25-27 NIV

Because we are fallible human beings, we worry. Even though we, as Christians, have the assurance of salvation—even though we, as Christians, have the promise of God's love and protection—we find ourselves fretting over the countless details of everyday life. Jesus understood our concerns when He spoke the reassuring words found in the sixth chapter of Matthew.

Perhaps you are concerned about the inevitable changes that have come as a result of your profession. Perhaps you are uncertain about your future, your relationships, or your finances. Or perhaps you are simply a "worrier" by nature. If so, make Matthew 6 a regular part of your daily Bible reading. This beautiful passage will remind you that God still sits in His heaven and you are His beloved child. Then, perhaps, you will worry a little less and trust God a little more, and that's as it should be because God is trustworthy . . . and you are protected.

I've read the last page of the Bible.
It's all going to turn out all right.

Billy Graham

Be anxious for nothing, but in everything
by prayer and supplication, with thanksgiving,
let your requests be made known to God.

Philippians 4:6 NKJV

Don't let worry rob you of the joy that
is rightfully yours. God is in heaven,
and He knows your every need. Focus on God
and His provisions, and watch gratefully as
the worries of today begin to fade away.

Jim Gallery

Any concern that is too small to be turned
into a prayer is too small to be made
into a burden.

Corrie ten Boom

Forgive me, Lord, when I worry. Worry reflects
a lack of trust in Your ability to meet my every
need. Help me to work, Lord, and not to worry.
And, keep me mindful, Father, that nothing,
absolutely nothing, will happen this day that
You and I cannot handle together.

—Amen—

My Prayer for Today

A Prayer for . . .

The Courage to Discipline

Discipline yourself for the purpose of godliness.
1 Timothy 4:7 NASB

As leaders of the classroom, we are charged with teaching discipline and, on occasion, dispensing it. We do so in the hopes that our students will learn that disciplined behavior is at the very foundation of successful living.

God's Holy Word is clear: He commands His children (of all ages) to lead godly, responsible, disciplined lives. God does not reward irresponsibility, nor does He reward sloth. To the contrary, God has created a world that mirrors a well-run classroom: those who behave responsibly earn meaningful rewards, while those who behave irresponsibility invite swift punishment.

Wise teachers demonstrate the importance of discipline by their words and their actions. Wise students pay attention . . . and learn.

May you be a disciplined teacher, and may you give your students the environment that they deserve: a disciplined classroom.

Faith is stronger than fear.

John Maxwell

He who heeds discipline shows the way to life,
but whoever ignores correction
leads others astray.

Proverbs 10:17 NIV

Do not let Satan deceive you into
being afraid of God's plans for your life.

R. A. Torrey

Jesus Christ can make the weakest man
into a divine dreadnought, fearing nothing.

Oswald Chambers

A Prayer for Today

Heavenly Father, make me a teacher of
discipline and righteousness, and make me
a diligent teacher in the service of Your Son,
Christ Jesus. Let me teach others by the
faithfulness of my conduct, and let me follow
Your will and Your Word, today and every day.
—Amen—

My Prayer for Today

A Prayer for . . .

A Generous Spirit

Freely you have received, freely give.
Matthew 10:8 NIV

Kindness and generosity are woven into the fabric of the Christian faith. And, because we are important role models to our students, we have an obligation to demonstrate generosity, not only by our words but also by our deeds.

The words of Matthew 10:8 are clear: because we have received so much from our Creator, we are commanded to give freely to His children. As followers of Christ, we have been immeasurably blessed. In return, we must give generously of our time, our possessions, our testimonies, and our love.

Today and every day, let Christ's words be your guide and let His eternal love fill your heart. When you do, your stewardship will be a reflection of your love for Him, and that's exactly as it should be. After all, He loved you first.

Carry each other's burdens, and in this way
you will fulfill the law of Christ.

Galatians 6:2 NIV

Nothing is really ours until we share it.

C. S. Lewis

All the blessings we enjoy are divine deposits,
committed to our trust on this condition:
that they should be dispensed for
the benefit of our neighbors.

John Calvin

It is the duty of every Christian to be
Christ to his neighbor.

Martin Luther

Dear Lord, Your Word tells me that it is
more blessed to give than to receive.
Make me a faithful steward of the gifts
You have given me, and let me share
those gifts generously with others,
today and every day that I live.
—Amen—

My Prayer for Today

My Hopes & Prayers for Next Week

My Hopes & Prayers for Next Week

Day 22

A Prayer for . . .

The Wisdom to Laugh

There is a time for everything, and a season for every activity under heaven . . . a time to weep and a time to laugh, a time to mourn and a time to dance . . . .

Ecclesiastes 3:1, 4 NIV

Laughter is God's gift, and He intends that we enjoy it. Yet sometimes, because of the inevitable stresses of everyday life, laughter seems only a distant memory. As Christians we have every reason to be cheerful and to be thankful. Our blessings from God are beyond measure, starting, of course, with a gift that is ours for the asking, God's gift of salvation through Christ Jesus.

Few things in life are more absurd than the sight of a grumpy Christian. So today, as you go about your daily activities, approach life with a smile and a chuckle. After all, God created laughter for a reason . . . and Father indeed knows best. So laugh!

There is nothing that rejuvenates the parched,
delicate spirits of children faster than
when a lighthearted spirit pervades
the home and laughter fills its halls.

James Dobson

A keen sense of humor helps us to overlook
the unbecoming, understand the
unconventional, tolerate the unpleasant,
overcome the unexpected,
and outlast the unbearable.

Billy Graham

Nehemiah said, "Go and enjoy choice food
and sweet drinks, and send some to those
who have nothing prepared. This day is sacred
to our Lord. Do not grieve, for the joy
of the Lord is your strength."

Nehemiah 8:10 NIV

According to Jesus, it is God's will that
His children be filled with the joy of life.

Catherine Marshall

A Prayer for Today

Lord, when I begin to take myself or my life
too seriously, let me laugh. When I rush
from place to place, slow me down, Lord,
and let me laugh. Put a smile on my face,
Dear Lord, and let me share that smile with
all who cross my path . . . and let me laugh.

—Amen—

My Prayer for Today

A Prayer for . . .

Words That Are Pleasing to God

Let the words of my mouth, and the meditation of my heart, be acceptable in thy sight, O LORD, my strength and my redeemer.

Psalm 19:14 KJV

Think . . . pause . . . then speak: How wise is the teacher who can communicate in this way. But occasionally, amid the pressures of the school day, even the most considerate teacher may speak first and think next . . . with unfortunate results.

God's Word reminds us that "reckless words pierce like a sword, but the tongue of the wise brings healing" (Proverbs 12:18 NIV). If we seek to be a source of encouragement to our students, to our peers, and to our families, then we must measure our words carefully. Words are important: they can hurt or heal. Words can uplift us or discourage us, and reckless words, spoken in haste, cannot be erased.

Today, seek to encourage all who cross your path. Measure your words carefully. Speak wisely, not impulsively. Use words of kindness and praise, not words of anger or derision. Remember that you have the power to heal others or to injure them, to lift others up or to hold them back. When you lift them up, your wisdom will bring healing and comfort to a classroom and a world that needs both.

Fill the heart with the love of Christ
so that only truth and purity
can come out of the mouth.

Warren Wiersbe

To praise God is to please God.

Jim Gallery

God's Word is a light not only to our path but
to our thinking. Place it in your heart today,
and you will never walk in darkness.

Joni Eareckson Tada

Set a guard, O LORD, over my mouth;
Keep watch over the door of my lips.

Psalm 141:3 NASB

Lord, You have commanded me to choose
my words carefully so that I might be a source
of encouragement and hope to all whom I meet.
Keep me mindful, Father, that I have influence
on many people, especially my students . . .
make me an influence for good. And may
the words that I speak today be worthy
of the One who has saved me forever.

—Amen—

My Prayer for Today

Day 24

A Prayer for . . .

Optimism and Faith

For God has not given us a spirit of fearfulness,
but one of power, love, and sound judgment.

2 Timothy 1:7 HCSB

Pessimism and Christianity don't mix. Why? Because Christians have every reason to be optimistic about life here on earth and life eternal. As C. H. Spurgeon observed, "Our hope in Christ for the future is the mainstream of our joy." But sometimes, we fall prey to worry, frustration, anxiety, or sheer exhaustion, and our hearts become heavy. What's needed is plenty of rest, a large dose of perspective, and God's healing touch, but not necessarily in that order.

Today, make this promise to yourself and keep it: vow to be a hope-filled Christian. Think optimistically about your life, your profession, your future, and your students. Trust your hopes not your fears. Take time to celebrate God's glorious creation. And then, when you've filled your heart with hope and gladness, share your optimism with others. They'll be better for it, and so will you.

The essence of optimism is that it takes
no account of the present, but it is a source
of inspiration, of vitality, and of hope. Where
others have resigned, it enables a man to hold
his head high, to claim the future for himself,
and not abandon it to his enemy.

Dietrich Bonhoeffer

I can do everything through him
who gives me strength.

Philippians 4:13 NIV

The people whom I have seen succeed best
in life have always been cheerful and
hopeful people who went about their business
with a smile on their faces.

Charles Kingsley

Faith in faith is pointless. Faith in a living,
active God moves mountains.

Beth Moore

A Prayer for Today

Lord, let me be an expectant Christian.
Let me expect the best from You, and let
me look for the best in others. If I become
discouraged, Father, turn my thoughts and
my prayers to You. Let me trust You, Lord,
to direct my life. And, let me be Your faithful,
hopeful, optimistic servant every day that I live.
—Amen—

My Prayer for Today

Day 25

A Prayer for . . .

A Thankful Heart

Enter into His gates with thanksgiving,
And into His courts with praise.
Be thankful to Him, and bless His name.
For the LORD is good; His mercy is everlasting,
And His truth endures to all generations.

Psalm 100:4-5 NKJV

Thoughtful Christians are thankful Christians: As believing Christians, we are blessed beyond measure. God sent His only Son to die for our sins. And, by His grace, God has given us the priceless gifts of eternal love and eternal life. We, in turn, are instructed to approach our Heavenly Father with reverence and thanksgiving. But, as busy professionals caught between the rush of everyday living and the demands of the classroom, we may sometimes fail to pause and thank our Creator for His countless blessings.

When we slow down and express our gratitude to the One who made us, we enrich our own lives and the lives of those around us. Thanksgiving should become a habit, a regular part of our daily routines. Yes, God has blessed us beyond measure, and we owe Him everything, including our eternal praise.

Thanksgiving or complaining—these words
express two contrastive attitudes of the souls
of God's children in regard to His dealings
with them. The soul that gives thanks can find
comfort in everything; the soul that complains
can find comfort in nothing.

Hannah Whitall Smith

We ought to give thanks for all fortune:
if it is good, because it is good, if bad,
because it works in us patience, humility,
and the contempt of this world along with
the hope of our eternal country.

C. S. Lewis

Give thanks in all circumstances;
for this is God's will for you in Christ Jesus.

1 Thessalonians 5:18 NIV

God is in control, and therefore in everything
I can give thanks, not because of the situation,
but because of the One
who directs and rules over it.

Kay Arthur

A Prayer for Today

Heavenly Father, Your gifts are greater than
I can imagine. May I live each day with
thanksgiving in my heart and praise on my lips.
Thank You for the gift of Your Son and for
the promise of eternal life. Let me share
the joyous news of Jesus Christ, and let my life
be a testimony to His love and His grace.
—Amen—

My Prayer for Today

A Prayer for . . .

A Forgiving Heart

All bitterness, anger and wrath, insult
and slander must be removed from you,
along with all wickedness. And be kind
and compassionate to one another,
forgiving one another, just as God
also forgave you in Christ.

Ephesians 4:31-32 HCSB

Forgiveness is God's commandment, but oh how difficult a commandment it can be to follow. Being frail, fallible, imperfect human beings, we are quick to anger, quick to blame, slow to forgive, and even slower to forget. No matter. Forgiveness, although difficult, is God's way.

Teachers, having been placed in positions of leadership, serve as important role models to their students. As such, teachers must be models of forgiveness, both inside the classroom and out.

If there exists even one person, alive or dead, whom you have not forgiven (and that includes yourself), follow God's commandment and His will for your life: forgive. Hatred and bitterness and regret are not part of God's plan for your life. Forgiveness is.

Blessed are the merciful,
for they will be shown mercy.

Matthew 5:7 NIV

———

Looking back over my life, all I can see is mercy
and grace written in large letters everywhere.
May God help me have the same kind of heart
toward those who wound or offend me.

Jim Cymbala

———

Forgiveness is the precondition of love.

Catherine Marshall

———

Miracles broke the physical laws of
the universe; forgiveness broke the moral rules.

Philip Yancey

A Prayer for Today

Heavenly Father, sometimes I am tempted to strike out at those who have hurt me. Keep me mindful that forgiveness is Your commandment. You have forgiven me, Lord; let me show my thankfulness to You by offering forgiveness to others. And, when I do, may others see Your love reflected through my words and deeds.

—Amen—

My Prayer for Today

A Prayer for . . .

A Trusting Heart

In God have I put my trust:
I will not be afraid what man can do unto me.

Psalm 56:11 KJV

Where will you place your trust today? Will you trust in the ways of the world, or will you trust in the Word and the will of your Creator?

If you aspire to do great things for God's kingdom, you will trust Him completely.

Trusting God means trusting Him in every aspect of your life. You must trust Him with your relationships. You must trust Him with your finances. You must follow His commandments and pray for His guidance. Then, you can wait patiently for God's revelations and for His blessings.

When you trust your Heavenly Father without reservation, you can rest assured that in His own fashion and in His own time God will bless you in ways that you never could have imagined. So trust Him, and then prepare yourself for the abundance and joy that will most certainly be yours through Him.

True faith is man's weakness leaning
on God's strength.

D. L. Moody

—————

When we trust the author, we don't have to
know the story. We just know it will be true.

Gloria Gaither

—————

To you, O LORD, I lift up my soul.
I trust in you, my God.

Psalm 25:1 NLT

—————

Because God is my sovereign Lord, I was not
worried. He manages perfectly, day and night,
year in and year out, the movements of
the stars, the wheeling of the planets,
the staggering coordination of events that
go on at the molecular level in order to
hold things together. There is no doubt
that He can manage the timing
of my days and weeks.

Elisabeth Elliot

Lord, when I trust in the things of this earth,
I will be disappointed. But, when I put my faith
in You, I am secure. In every aspect of my life,
Lord, let me trust in Your boundless grace . . .
today, tomorrow, and forever.
—Amen—

My Prayer for Today

Day 28

A Prayer for . . .

Renewal

Come to Me, all you who are weary
and burdened, and I will give you rest.
Take My yoke upon you and learn from Me,
because I am gentle and humble in heart,
and you will find rest for your souls.
For My yoke is easy and My burden is light.

Matthew 11:28-30 HCSB

A Prayer for . . .

Even the most inspired Christian teachers can, from time to time, find themselves running on empty. The demands of daily life, combined with the stresses of the classroom, can drain us of our strength and rob us of the joy that is rightfully ours in Christ.

Are you tired or troubled? Turn your heart toward God in prayer. Are you weak or worried? Take the time—or, more accurately, make the time—to delve deeply into God's Holy Word. Are you spiritually depleted? Call upon fellow believers to support you, and call upon Christ to renew your spirit and your life. When you do, you'll discover that the Creator of the universe stands always ready and always able to create a new sense of wonderment and joy in you.

Therefore, if anyone is in Christ,
he is a new creation; old things have
passed away; behold,
all things have become new.

2 Corinthians 5:17 NKJV

Like a spring of pure water, God's peace
in our hearts brings cleansing and
refreshment to our minds and bodies.

Billy Graham

Jesus is calling the weary to rest,
Calling today, calling today,
Bring Him your burden and you shall be blest;
He will not turn you away.

Fanny Crosby

A Prayer for Today

Lord, sometimes, the responsibilities of teaching can be demanding indeed. When I feel tired or discouraged, let me turn my thoughts and my prayers to You. Let me always trust Your promises, Father, and let me draw strength from those promises and from Your unending love.

—Amen—

My Prayer for Today

My Hopes & Prayers for Next Week

My Hopes & Prayers for Next Week

Day 29

A Prayer for . . .

Today

This is the day which the LORD has made;
let us rejoice and be glad in it.

Psalm 118:24 NASB

The familiar words of Psalm 118 remind us that today, like every day, is a priceless gift from God. And as teachers, we are doubly blessed: we can celebrate the glory of God's creation and we can celebrate the precious students that He has entrusted to our care.

What do you expect from the day ahead? Are you expecting God to do wonderful things, or are you living beneath a cloud of apprehension and doubt. Do you expect God to use you in unexpected ways, or do you expect another uneventful day to pass with little fanfare? As a thoughtful believer, the answer to these questions should be obvious.

For Christian believers, every new day offers exciting possibilities. God's Word promises that Christ has come to this earth to give us abundant life and eternal salvation. We, in turn, should respond to God's gifts by treasuring each day and using our time here on earth to glorify our Creator and share the Good News of His Son.

Each day is a special gift from God, a treasure to be savored and celebrated. May we—as believers who have so much to celebrate—never fail to praise our Creator by rejoicing in His glorious creation.

Today is mine. Tomorrow is none of
my business. If I peer anxiously into the fog of
the future, I will strain my spiritual eyes so that
I will not see clearly what is required of me now.

Elisabeth Elliot

Wherever you are, be all there.
Live to the hilt every situation
you believe to be the will of God.

Jim Elliot

Encourage one another daily,
as long as it is called Today . . . .

Hebrews 3:13 NIV

God gave you this glorious day.
Don't disappoint Him. Use it for His glory.

Marie T. Freeman

A Prayer for Today

Lord, You have given me another day of life;
let me celebrate this day, and let me use it
according to Your plan. I praise You, Father, for
my life and for the friends, family members, and
students who make it rich. Enable me to live
each moment to the fullest as I give thanks for
Your creation, for Your love, and for Your Son.
—Amen—

My Prayer for Today

Day 30

A Prayer for . . .

Our Children

Then He took a child, had him stand among them, and taking him in His arms, He said to them, "Whoever welcomes one little child such as this in My name welcomes Me. And whoever welcomes Me does not welcome Me, but Him who sent Me."

Mark 9:36-37 HCSB

Every child is different, but every child is similar in this respect: he or she is a priceless gift from the Father above. And, with the Father's gift come immense responsibilities for parents and teachers alike. Even on those difficult days when the classroom is in an uproar and the papers are piled to the ceiling, wise teachers never forget the overriding goal of their profession: shaping young minds. The very best teachers shape those minds with love, with discipline, and with God.

Our children are our most precious resource. May we, as responsible Christians and dedicated teachers, pray for children here at home and for children around the world. Every child is God's child. May we, as concerned adults, behave— and pray—accordingly.

I have no greater joy than this,
to hear of my children walking in the truth.

3 John 1:4 NASB

Let us look upon our children;
let us love them and train them as children
of the covenant and children of the promise.
These are the children of God.

Andrew Murray

When Jesus put the little child in the midst
of His disciples, He did not tell the little child
to become like His disciples; He told
the disciples to become like the little child.

Ruth Bell Graham

Kids go where there is excitement.
They stay where there is love.

Zig Ziglar

Today, Dear Lord, I pray for all Your children.
This world holds countless dangers and
temptations. I pray that our children may
be protected from harm, and that they may
discover Your will, Your love, and Your Son.
—Amen—

My Prayer for Today

Day 31
A Prayer for . . .
God's Love

For God so loved the world, that he gave his
only begotten Son, that whosoever believeth in
him should not perish, but have everlasting life.

John 3:16 KJV

God's love changes lives. And as Christian teachers who have received the priceless gift of God's grace, we must make certain that our students can clearly see the changes that God has made in us. Can we be perfect teachers? Of course not. Can we, at all times, be patient, kind, calm, and loving? That's highly unlikely. What we can do is this: we can demonstrate to our students that Christ's love does indeed make a difference in the lives of those who accept Him as their Savior.

God's grace is the ultimate gift, and we owe Him the ultimate in thanksgiving. Let us praise the Creator for His priceless gift, let us share His Good News, and let us live according to His commandments. When we do, our students will be blessed with powerful, godly role models. And we teachers will be transformed not only for a day but also for all eternity.

Jesus loves us with fidelity, purity,
constancy, and passion,
no matter how imperfect we are.

Stormie Omartian

God loves each of us as if
there were only one of us.

St. Augustine

Jesus: the proof of God's love.

Philip Yancey

Lord, Your love is infinite and eternal.
Although I cannot fully understand
the depths of Your love, I can praise it,
return it, and share it . . .
today and every day.
—Amen—

My Prayer for Today

My Hopes & Prayers for Next Month

My Hopes & Prayers for Next Month

My Hopes & Prayers for Next Month

My Hopes & Prayers for Next Month

*Selected
Scripture*

Behavior

Even a child is known by his actions,
by whether his conduct is pure and right.
Proverbs 20:11 NIV

———

Therefore, get your minds ready for action,
being self-disciplined, and set your hope
completely on the grace to be brought
to you at the revelation of Jesus Christ.
As obedient children, do not be conformed
to the desires of your former ignorance but,
as the One who called you is holy,
you also are to be holy in all your conduct.
1 Peter 1:13-15 HCSB

———

A good person produces good deeds from
a good heart, and an evil person produces
evil deeds from an evil heart.
Whatever is in your heart
determines what you say.
Luke 6:45 NLT

You see that a person is justified
by what he does
and not by faith alone.

James 2:24 NIV

Miracles

You are the God who performs miracles; you display your power among the peoples.

Psalm 77:14 NIV

God verified the message by signs and wonders and various miracles and by giving gifts of the Holy Spirit whenever he chose to do so.

Hebrews 2:4 NLT

Jesus said to them, "I have shown you many great miracles from the Father."

John 10:32 NIV

That is what the Scriptures mean when they say, "No eye has seen, no ear has heard, and no mind has imagined what God has prepared for those who love him."

1 Corinthians 2:9 NLT

For with God nothing
shall be impossible.

Luke 1:37 KJV

Teaching

Fix these words of mine in your hearts
and minds. Teach them to your children,
talking about them when you sit at home
and when you walk along the road,
when you lie down and when you get up.

Deuteronomy 11:18-19 NIV

———

Do not neglect the gift that is in you.

1 Timothy 4:14 NKJV

———

God has given each of us the ability to do
certain things well. So if God has given you the
ability to prophesy, speak out when you have
faith that God is speaking through you. If your
gift is that of serving others, serve them well.
If you are a teacher, do a good job of teaching.
If your gift is to encourage others,
do it! If you have money, share it generously.
If God has given you leadership ability,
take the responsibility seriously.
And if you have a gift for showing
kindness to others, do it gladly.

Romans 12:6-8 NKJV

Be gentle to all,
able to teach, patient.

2 Timothy 2:24 NKJV

Anger

All bitterness, anger and wrath, insult and slander must be removed from you, along with all wickedness. And be kind and compassionate to one another, forgiving one another, just as God also forgave you in Christ.

Ephesians 4:31-32 HCSB

I want men everywhere to lift up holy hands in prayer, without anger or disputing.

1 Timothy 2:8 NIV

If anyone considers himself religious and yet does not keep a tight rein on his tongue, he deceives himself and his religion is worthless.

James 1:26 NIV

For God hath not appointed us to wrath, but to obtain salvation by our Lord Jesus Christ . . . .

1 Thessalonians 5:9 KJV

A fool gives full vent
to his anger, but a wise man
keeps himself under control.

Proverbs 29:11 NIV

Worry

Don't worry about anything; instead,
pray about everything. Tell God what you need,
and thank him for all he has done.

Philippians 4:6 NLT

For this reason I say to you, do not be worried
about your life, as to what you will eat
or what you will drink; nor for your body, as to
what you will put on. Is not life more than food,
and the body more than clothing? Look at
the birds of the air, that they do not sow, nor
reap nor gather into barns, and yet
your heavenly Father feeds them.
Are you not worth much more than they?

Matthew 6:25-26 HCSB

Trust in him at all times, O people;
pour out your hearts to him,
for God is our refuge.

Psalm 62:8 NIV

Let not your heart be troubled;
you believe in God,
believe also in Me.

John 14:1 NKJV